AF591372

the syndrome papers

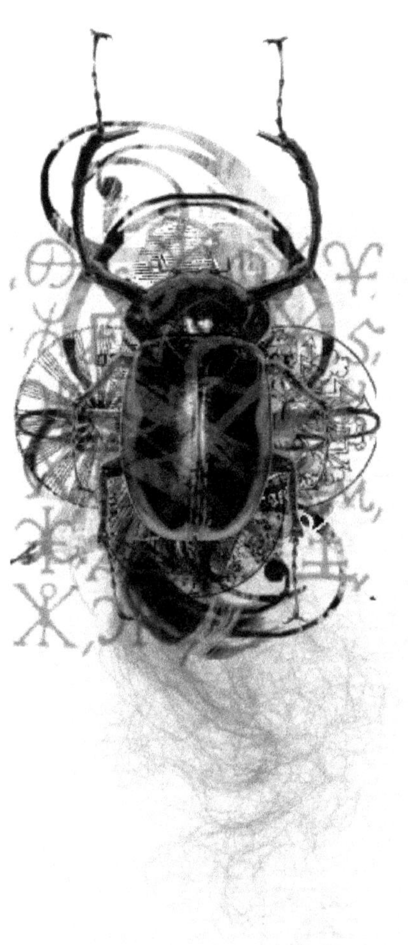

the syndrome papers

by Bryan McLean

This is a work of fiction. All incidents, dialogue, and characters portrayed are products of the author's imagination and are not to be construed as real. Any similarity, without satiric intent, to actual events or persons living or dead is purely coincidental.

Cover and book design by Bryan McLean.

Cover image and all contained artwork and design by Bryan McLean.

*Spanish versions of "*Snow*", titled* "Nieve"*, and "Little Wings", titled* "Pequeñas Alas"*, were edited in part by Valery Santillana and Luisa Garzon.*

McLean, Bryan, 1977 -

The Syndrome Papers / Bryan McLean

Poems

ISBN – 978-1-257-62628-1

www.lyinghere.com

1 1 2 3 5 8 1 3 2 1 4 4

Limited Printing.

My strangers, my readers, my masses, these words and manuscript are dedicated to you. Your silent uncertainty and understanding of our shared late night concerns will keep our weary heads and thoughts forming our mutual unity.

We hold each other up against the odds.

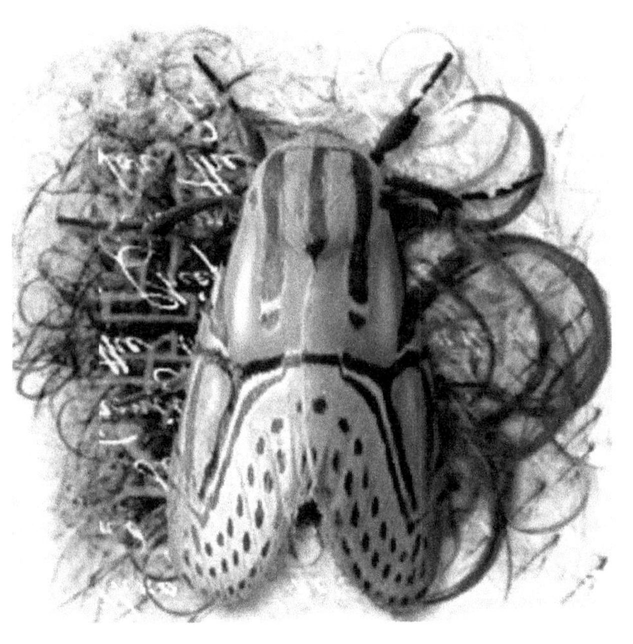

book i : the dark transmutations in our night time

book ii : the alchemal quandary

book iii : the epoch wake

book i : the dark transmutations in our night time

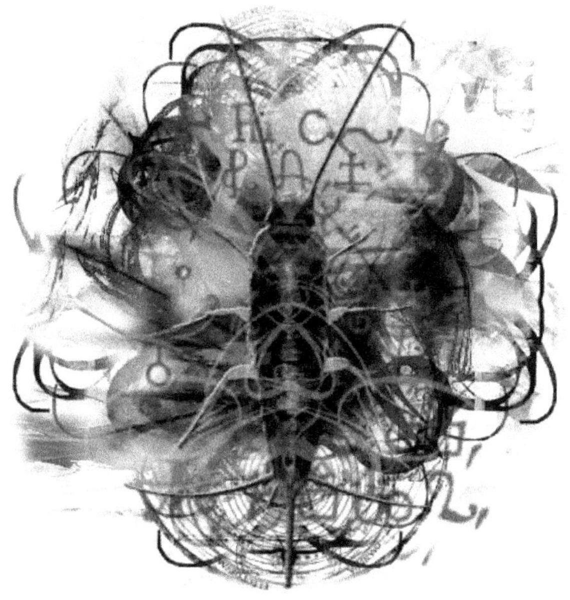

" manifestos are weakening in your skin
your convictions are losing out
and every dark mark
that mars your precious surface
turns up listless in these late hours
that are running out on us "

[.the.night.monsters.]

and I'm running
cause it's on the page
and my knees
are scraped and burning
bleeding from the rub

and when I find my way out
I will finally be done with all of this
the fending of the night monsters
and the beings still familiar
with the underside of my bed

but there is no living here
only running
only now here
in our night time
the dreaming spaces
that we are all
far too familiar with

familiar as the last time
a specific friend is near
their memory clasped
in your hands and head
still shaking with weakening clarity
between the secret leaking worlds
of just me and you

[.wanting.words.]

no words equal
the wounds we wear
it masks our scarring
and blurs our edges
that are slowly cutting into us

where you hear my name
in the russet of wind
pushing at your lobes
under sky and skein
infinitely smaller
than the last strand
or finger tip
that touched you

harsh are my razor words
that lack sincerity
in every wanting way
and you strain to hear
all the things
trapped inside my head

where nighttime only knows
the hushed varied tones
of your simplistic sighs
up against my side
your hands holding me down
where wing & brow
furrow from the upset thoughts
that mark and mar our sleep

[.awake.all.burnt.]

no eyes
rotting words
on the blotted page
all my marker
buried here
it's out on the mile
in the sounding gun
the one left out in white sand

my echoes
ever reaching
all directions
make my sounds surround
in swirling serpentine edge

still down here

under wing
still flightless
in your hollow heart
my burnings turn me numb
and I cannot hear the sounds
I make in these empty rooms
all this night time

the spirits drunk
or burnt from too much acid
my echoes reaching
at the dark edges of my space
where we lay our palms to ground
now head near door
angry in your summer light

now long forgotten
but still tearing at the faces
that make up the watching sounds

all our night eyes
gone out
blown out
and only our hollow sounds
replace the movements
they once made
in the dark late day

where shifting toes
reach broken boards
and sleep refuses
to find me here
nothing will put me down
nor out
inconsequential
and so accustomed
to my lack of rest

your hands break my shelter
and there is no movement now
only the ache
and angry edges
of my tangled house
harrowed by your head & hands
in bindings and short writings
that I find in letter format
under my blatant run through
abandoned now for my only calling

[.the.hollow.future.]

under the pillow
under handed
your lacking racer's heat
is eating up our light
and dismantling our sun
where we cancel our fears
to match our needful freedom
where there is no palm
holding us up any longer

tired of cupping under-chin
to distract your attentive
back on me
in song works
all my weary nights
keep finding at my empty core
the hollow hearted future
that's wrought
with my bidden palms
that show spires in the glass

rubbing matchlings at twilight
our senses know the other worlds
you can see the ugly faces
that all mark the coming days
with their hungry breath
and drooling jaws
that's blurring up our semblance
and rending down our seems

but you're apart
in mirrors like your memory
where it seethes
in the thunderland
that’s fading from our tones

lengthy are our shadows here
as we stand on watch
and know all dirt & dust
as familiar as a friend
are aching to hold us
in our freshly ready resting places
underneath our waiting feet

[.you.wrote.]

sacred knowing
in our angry placebo egos
ghosts are our natural state
outside meat & breath
where our enemies lie
and all our lies
are waking

in the nighttime edges
where we seethe
they no longer require us
to hold them down
and make their lungs move

in the underground shifting
our masks are
all that are holding us back
from making the shaking words
echo out in our lingering seconds
so that in piecemeal breaks
thunder knows our names

in shapes of sound
that drum against my cured face
its pressing down
and there is no wherewithal left
to feed us all the breathy love
that's murmuring our endings
and kissing down our spines

feeling at our weary edges
only seen from bright blue
or sea grey green
it's our limit to the nail
scuffing into the boards

our wrappings all waxed
and now etched with lines
from your whirring passion
that's now pressed heavily
into my fore running skin
as epic as the lines you wrote

[.pequeñas.alas.]

pequeñas alas
baten contra
vidrio y ventrículo
contra los bordes frisados
pero falta poco para el silencio
pequeño es sagrado
en tus varios
tonos escondidos
mientras palabras derraman
fuera de tus labios
y más allá de tu boca
tan lista a beber
pequeñas palabras que tú piensas
que no puedo decir

[.little.wings.]

little wings
beat against
pane & ventricle
against frosted edges
but little is still to silent
little is sacred
in your varied
hushed tones
as words still spill
out of your lips
and past your mouth
so set for drinking
little words you think
that I cannot say

[.pushing.echoes.]

my king and cutting
are still down here
where nothing is real
nothing we are keeping
or holding out on
as it's easier to put it up
all those things for granted
up against the radio skies

and those marks
that we all still have
running down our cheeks
built from the forms of memories
which are switching our faces
like pushing echoes
of your grace and giving

but I'm not hiding in this skin
no, just keeping myself
barely above your water
that's rushing to drown us down
fighting to keep my works
from brimming over
in this stirring silence
that's rising up to meet
our final counting hours

[.chai.]

a thousand deaths
every night
during dreams
so that in waking
a thousand lives
will come

[.the.imaginary.boy.]

the world once had
beneath bare feet
and barren chests
falling away steadily
our only steady thing
the gravity here
all from his dis ease
is still an empty echo
tearing at flesh and cinders
eating inside out

feathers all gone now
stolen in the dry winter rush
there is no beating left
at his side nor in his head
of lashes that know
intangible wonder
where he is shaking
to turn it all off from burning

the horror of a wordless world
where no one feels what he can
where sight is near gone
and he holds face
so sternly like you'd want it
to finish those writings and siennas

still pulling at seams
that he wanted to work at
which keep breaking
and are all promised out
snapping, no matter how hard
they kept being arranged
knowing the lines won't stop
marking pale cheeks

invisible to the bone
one of many
just one face more
that couldn't be shown off
number one or not
his strings cut down
underneath the night
knowing his hands
won't work anymore at being

all in grey boy
because that's his colour
bright as his last shining day
laid out in late light
his drinking not working
no words filling apparitions
his cutting scrawlings empty still
showing only out the window sill
how faceless he will always be

[.the.man.of.the.hours.]

gun to the ballet floor
he's handed one down
in his stitch up riot suit
against the shine and lack luster
used to wake us
from our burning time
where we walk in fevered segments
under blankets
sweaty and swollen
with our prone figures

his eyes are groping out
hands on every ugly surface now
reaching each curve
each contour speaking out
just to him
smoothing out deftly
freshly showered surfaces
all supple for the taking

roaming over the room
he's your david
all in stereo
sculpted cleanly on the sides
rough lines gone
but still massing
at your rebel table
holding down the watch-works
on our plates and pander

cannot anymore place it
in its eloquence
our writhing words
all hollowed out now
where he knows

our flaccid intent
is on display
just like he knows you
all gory insides out

but he's watching
smoking from his wall
our every beaten step
slipping as our heads drop
and the lies keep longer
steaming from our mouths
that touch with aching breath

holding on
until they cut me down
in all my gory glory
soaked through
bindings still clear
and cutting
at my sides & shoulders
are the words you've used
just to tie me up here
the ones he's written down for record
jotting in his little books & scraps
under brim where his eyes only know

it works every hour
my head never stops
because it knows
every footprint behind me
is his in turn and in time

figured I'd go out loud
but it's all so quiet
still empty of any peace
only his breathing
is tracing my awareness

as it echoes off of edges
and makes new sounds
that are so familiar

those shapely sounds
drowning me heavily
under thick memories
that thought could be traded
for one more shining day

where hands keep everything
right in its aching place
away from the man
that watches my hours
from inside skin, lip, and lid

[.girl.with.words.]

do you read what you write baby?
or is it just a functionary regime
that your fingers take flight with
against the thoughts that keep you
marking out your guess work
that edges in or echoes outside
of the lines you keep lending
that seem so much like truths
that just can't be for real
even when your singing is down
in heavy lines on the paper
you keep carrying with you

[.transmutations.]

grown accustomed
to the dark time
in lightless rooms
every corner shifts
items scuddling & crawling
outside the periphery
they still lie

all legs and lines
second dimensions & awkward
too plain to see
here all of our
dark transmutations find us
they know each fault & facet
all gleaned from our faces

each depiction
one of angry seconds
and weary losses
hands cannot touch
aching to be
crawling out from undersides
feeding needless fear

all at clocking hours
works bring us home
sleeping deeply
all shapes formed inside
sucking or crawling their way
into existence

their terrible needs hungry
beyond comprehension
what we have been building
our black sun burning
rending us shapeless
under their glaring eyes

[.the.pushing.street.]

in dreaming
this is the world
that's lived in
the soft wet night
where fog still touches
the lamp light

sickly warmth still
pushes at my weary face
here at my crossroads
hungered down underneath
my driving needs
wrenching out

my snickersnack
against your drowning sounds
that cloud my night sky
so near to me
as it tries desperately
to hold me down
(kissingly to the earth)

[.touching.]

your mouth corners and caters
to your every whim
like we all would
succumbing in your echoing light
that is shifting against
your warming surfaces
in your aching palms
that rest against my cold chest
in the middle of the night

[.last.gaze.]

working so hard
just to be
your face in the crowd
the echoes
are in D minor
just underneath your skin
where its burning
and my hands
are no match
for the seething hate
I'm sure you have for me
underneath
your burning gaze

[.my.side.]

foot falls
in the silent places
where echoes of
our breaking humanity
seems thin and frail
when pressed against
your unnerving
perfect skin
that I miss so much
against my side

[.nine.tuesdays.out.]

cutting below this
where we rest
because we are all in so deep
and can't breathe our breath out
without the late hours
to cure us warmly
and keep us aimed homeward

bound down in sounds
we make at breaking lights
where the traffic flickers
under fog heavy ruin
and fat waiting lines
that run the length of glass
that's keeping your faces back

handfuls of little lit bombs
like weighted moth mounds
that are bulging and shifting
and eager to flee
from my finger tips
and cutting nails
sadly knowing all this time
that they could have built me better

where your face is glowing
still wet from the early air
that's making all these stinging eyes
turn from frown and away
missing your burdened lines
that streak and coarse down
harshly finding each cracked edge
that's in my holding wake

[.red.]

it is in red
now all read out
the words your mouth
have wrapped around
right on the wall for showing
that I've been watching
with my heart watching
in the dark lined light
where no one sleeps

because between these hours
and underneath these sheets
there is still nothing and no one
that straightens me out
where I am just one more boy
in caked cadmium words
that are never fixed
nor mended deeply
just waiting on your self

still the red light is down
burning through my window
eating up the remnants
of all the things I've been
and recouping very little
of the steady thunder
that's been mixed too thickly
in our remitting transmissions
to even hear us out now

where the recluse checks his watch
and realizes that all these minutes
are just one more crimson edge
that is carving deeply and straight
into our seemingly endless grooves

book ii : the alchemal quandary

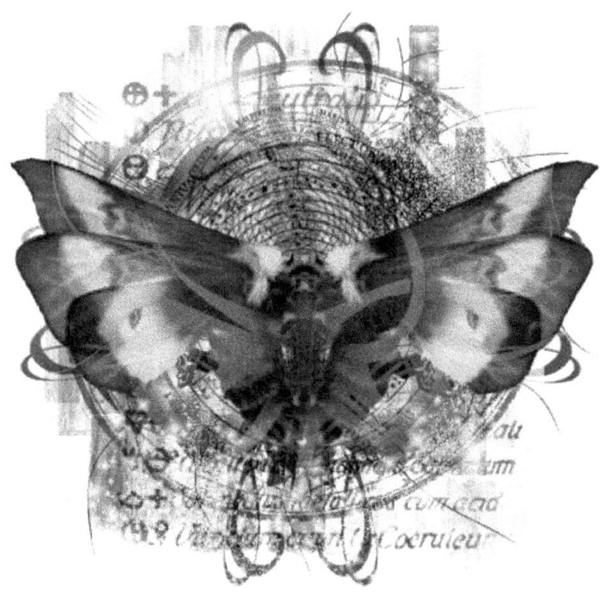

" it's in our nighttime masses
manifesting in your skin
the angles and awkward glances
coming from your naked-numb body
sprawled still in your exposed cocoon "

[.the.living.night.]

hearing forms from
the hollow halls
only at these hours
do we sit and wait
on mattresses that know
no more hands nor hate
only tired hushed sounds
of dormant conversations
we have dropped
at the bedroom door

[.the.living.night.ii.]

every minute counting down
counting out against us now
watchworks know
our every meaningless second
hands all spread out
across smalls of backs
and hips that press back down
gasping scratching at the eardrum
fighting to keep breath
to stay above the undertow
soakingly sucking down
into the nighttime surfaces

[.the.living.night.iii.]

just rest now
cupping small frames
out against
exhausted styles
laid out in livid angles
knuckles fallen back
over chests crested
with heavy sighs
and enigmatic grins
all hidden underneath
the knowing shadows
of the room we're in

[.the.damage.in.our.right.and.wrong.]

just all those little things
that still lay
between two people
lovers friends acquaintances
the damage in our right and wrong
without song on the knife blade
that's where our broken slumber lies

under all this skirting
not prepared
the wind my kind & cruel foe
its message clear
echoes from the outskirts
where the wild girls lie

but it's still there
where you are not
running all the night hours
tired but I cannot sleep
every aching moment
is acting out again

[.nieve.]

nunca cualquier cosa entre nosotros
excepto estas millas
estos cielos
y camas
donde las muchachas acuestan y calumnian
donde todo es en espera
y tú me dices
necesito reposar, respirar
mientras te inclinas contra mi lado ardiente
pero mi boca se esquina
porque mi cabeza no duerme
sin importarle lo que tú digas
y yo núnca tomo fotos
porque finjo
que vuelvo
todas las fotografías que derramo
hasta en mi dormir
que nunca vendrá por mí
ningunas manos empujando hacia mí

[.snow.]

never anything between us
except these miles
these skies
and beds
where girls lie and lay
where it’s all in wait

and you tell me
I need to rest, to breathe
as you lean against my burning side
but my mouth corners
because my head won't sleep
no matter what you say

and I never take photos
because I pretend
I'm coming back
all the photographs I shed
even in all my sleep
that’s never coming for me
no hands pushing for me

[.through.the.park.]

it's not right, brother
that in morning
we pass in parting
me in my long grey coat
that's hugging at the wind
and at evening end
we greet in park's late light
you on your bench
stained red t-shirt
dirty as your denim
bottle down, now unclenched love
right arm gone
and last hand mangled

[.late.nite.leaking.]

it’s late nite
still leaking
and no words
are coming out
thoughts all gone
like breath and wind
and I cannot stop shaking

four a.m.
making it harder
just can't rest
when so many others
need holding up
to keep us all in place
for just one more moment
outside your hands
that know no bounds

[.our.vanities.]

drenched in night
sky falling
trees drooping lower
where we are not dying
we simply cannot see
the wind that's rending
our edges round
and the humming in the dark
reminds our memories
of the soaked late hour
this really is

[.not.our.luxury.]

it’s not our
luxury,
my love,
to lay in bed
with the world
turning
against us

[.v.&.v.]

how hilarious
    no sounds
out against you
    & your love
scratching & crawling
at your side,
    faithful &
forgotten,
underfoot are
the remnants of
ventricle & valve

[.as.the.numb.light.goes.]

amicably, ardently
we go down
in black taxicabs
and hurling perils
sounding in chimes
our seasonal rush

nighttime all encumbered
in your sentimental vows
faithfully we're running
to slam the door

I think it's all locked out
and run down
echoes to our empty boots
hearts not longing anymore

the numb light goes out
it's in all the things unsaid
and without your doubt
written in the snow
I might still know my name

[.lovers, I.]

like teeth tucked back
hidden in the shelter of gum & maw
where it's one more for the lovers
in their six o'clock shroud
nothing cuts more
than ending a sleepless night
in the rising a.m.

[.clenching.mine.]

gray matter
and the stain & strain
of broad daylight
slicing through
each slit of window
it's cutting my patience
where hands only shudder
over our eyelids in the dark
and drain down fingers
over cheek, bone, & lips
these fingers
that miss your palms
clenching mine

[.nite.and.skin.]

all the lights
out in the night
are watching slits
(observers watching)

lamp posts preen down
seedy traffic & guttural tail lights
feasting and burning up
heavy sky to wet street

far off dirty dull bulbs
in apartment kitchens
look questioningly
at you and me

all these cuts glaring back
their sharpening sentience and
spear like eyelashes are hungry
prepared to rend meat from bone

impatiently waiting
their stark naked glare
so fresh on your supple
nitemare skin

[.turning.]

base metals at work
in our marriages
in our shifting
all underneath
these mechanisms
you've managed to build up
all around you
serpentine gears winding
to meet your weary
laid out feet

[.the.silence.eaters.]

hungry ghosts love mornings
the gaps in between
where no sounds
meet our lips

hungry echoes
consume our bridging silence
where everything goes unsaid
at these early
unbroken hours

nothing we can do
but feed their hungry minutes
each pocket unfilled
empty spaces
to gaps we make

hushed to humming
against your sides
all odds out
and unfriendly

riding at our closed lips
and misdirecting eyes
that shift to each
empty sentence
that fails & falls short
of our breathless maw

[.depending.]

may still lose you
in time
the free hand
running from the still
the hour depicts
it's never too late
only too long
until our next pass
in the dimming light

[.lips.too.close.]

the city lit like candles
and neon rushing red
my mouth is full of you

where there is only
biting and nails left
for us to communicate with

as the lights in our
windowlined back drop
shrouds our secrets
and our needful touch

book iii : the epoch wake

" marching, hungry eyes
reach every facet of your brittle skin
meta-phoria gliding over your rough,
encumbered surfaces
that manifest in your clouded iris "

[.last night, l.]

branches cutting still
palms run from bleeding
leaking at the lines
ground down
all my girls
still cutting deep
their cackles and chains
no longer scratching
at my weakening memory

[.props.for.august.]

thinking that this place
has burned us down
turned us out
against each other

and the matchsticks crawling
in candle light
are the only sentinels
on watch this hour

trying to be active
aching from need
games like russian roulette
with our threadbear hearts
out to the point of no return

where I don't think
I can do it anymore
rolling on the wheel
of love or lust

[.calling.]

call rape
in the barren wastes
hypocrisy in our humanity
where we are down here
nine and five and howling

under here
our calling
on the knife point
cluttered up and sundered
in our quiet raging dawn

[.zen.hands.]

we cannot know
every rain drop's destiny
we can merely hold
only a few in our hand

[.tonite, I.]

the keys are tracking
pulling strings
hum & echo uniquely gliding
mostly shaping their
rotting tune or tone
where we rub eyes
at the stinging hours
pounding out the notes
left open and wanting
doors that close
or rub our knuckles bare

skin curvaceous, supple
pulling strings
our valves smashing
sussing out en route
every endeavor
that devours
our leaking hours
leaking lines down
your scrubby bare faces
and raving stark stares
glaring back out from
behind glass encampments
and thin lined kitchenettes

knees, bent to begging
pulling strings
hands holding heads
in weeping motions
that our bodies are inclined to
naturally our gravity
curves our bending spines

the marching anti-bodies
no, body
grinding
down to nine and five
& my cutting skills
demeaned, pander-less
underneath this place
but I'm so uneasy
with your daunting faces
glaring back at me

[.in.empty.rooms.]

sleepless
numb from anger
knife-eyed and dulling
under a.m. lights
in empty rooms
filled with books & notes
all surround
the burning frustration
its gravity knows me
still not my place
to wait nor wonder
cannot shake this feeling
my avoidance in slumber
knowing all my guise
will follow me there

[.cutting.love.]

girls all wolves
and I'm running free
cuz your cutting love
is so apparent
weakening my prestige
lurking in my beautiful spite
that's so clear
on my sundering skin

[.tián.cǎo.]

.i.

a thousand years
sweetgrass strands
blowing lonely
without you

.ii.

wild anticipation
palpations
greet your feet
stirring at your
masterful ankles
& cumbersome toes

[.seems.in.your.skin.]

under eternal twilight
star shine pisses down
to put out the fires
glowing in our hot
incandescent bellies

hundreds of riddles glow
off your seething skin
and your tempered hands
washing over me again
nudging at my tendrils
protruding from my core

angry with your smashed
lamplight & sundered skin
pouring from your frothing lips
limbs still splintered
in your empty alleyways
occipitals crumpled at the frame
moths lying like burnt panels
against the seems in your skin

[.basin.]

the sun is reaching me
but the girls are cutting me
and in the thunder
of our culture
I am still breaking

yet still-sounds are singing
up from your basin
where echoes
reach your surface
through your washing hands
that reach the lines
still streaming
down your cheeks

[.better.set.]

no sleep
it's all our
late hour
echoes
that haunt me
all my works laid out
better set to burning
in our empty hours
that keep on bleeding through
but no one hears me out here
where words just stay like wind

[.drown.me.]

drown me
in all your weary words
that aren't reaching me
as I'm begging
to hear you again
just one more
precious syllable again
because my strings aren't real
and nothing is holding me
nor keeping me up any longer

[.sidelines.]

madness my compass now
down here
where all children
are withered
from the eye
of media pedagogues

my weakening words
the ripples on
the cascading rivers
eating up the gaps
in between
salient sure moments

[.panacea.]

don't think she knows
that I'm down here
no recognition
on our sober slabs
under what should have been
the garish & glorious sun

yet turned out to be
heat lamps in series & sequence
we are one of many
and our shells do nothing
for all this drizzle
under november squalls

even now
I have all sorts
of words & works laid out
in all surround
all memento mori
like smoking congenital ghosts
that still linger
from all my younger days

rough & weary
but unknowingly we go
in and out of sorrow
like cafes & shoppes
in winter scenes

where here I'm far from sleeping
and my consciousness
is all that I have with me
everyone's doubts & shadows
all pushing at my head

no flex of wing
is curing this nothing
that we wake to
nor will it fill
my empty skin

[.echoes.in.jazz.&.blue.]

suffocating under
your jazz & scratch
the beat too narrow
where it's making us angry
in our late nite breaks

nothing that our hands touch
or could ever
lay themselves on
will make all of these
limitations go away

the echoes are in
my jazz & blue
where every second
is coming out
against our memories
eating up our precious time

still seeing
every fraction
of your terrible disease
stealing your purposeless beauty

out in front
like its ripe & ready
instead of your building
internal decay

[.burnt.petals.]

candid lines
in loveless skin
sweltering impatience
is running the late nite show

dusting from the trees
bloom petals falling
on your serene vellum
the subtlies irreplaceable
in all your supple creases

overshadowed, an alarming rate
one valve fights to shut
while others arise, racing
masses to our warfare fray

dark rooms still keep
all of our stroking secrets
palpations finding
all of our rounded-out edges

like seared thumbprints
one by one, conical
pressing softly
thousands of petals
into the small of your back

[.cadaver.secrets.]

claws at my dried lips
once meant for kissing
prying my mouth open
from the inside out
to crawl & gesture
jabbing out through
broken cheek & chin
clockwork beetles,
moths, and millipedes
love, each and every one
seeking out the heat of light
escaping the warmth
of an internal night
where rushing skin
has now gone cold

[.notorious.relations.]

searing, fleeting apathy
it's your edgeless sorrows
filling up these rooms
with dirty, empty lust
wordless, consistently mocking
corners of every flat
every surface that you touch

the aching air
straining notorious relations
all these phrases
sour contraptions built for feeling
things we cannot break you with
always out of our reach, on purpose

falling short
the words, the breath
you eek out, letters left out
that prove undoubtedly
how infinitesimally small
your hands really are

[.the.cutting.scenes.]

cut to size
cut to scene
on the floor
in strips, not in polaroid
all the damage in your skin
that won't rub out
your caustic lives
still blowing through
the black veins

plundered by our nature
the social scene cuts
out of labour or our passion
legacy is love
built to burnout
fading in your tripwires
and filthy alleyways

all in the crowd
all the lovers
that have gone to ground
undiscovered
in memory, not in celluloid
I am the damage in your skin
knotting, cutting lines
against your taught surfaces
tangible to tasteless

we have no words
cut between us
from longing lips where
breathless lacerations
mark the hour
eyes just lay
on sundered skin

syndrome synopsis

The Syndrome Papers are a satire and study of our human nature and actions. We, as a wakening culture, come to terms with decisions and emotions often in our off hours, late at night, in the gaps between sleep and wakefulness. Often dark creatures linger there, created by our late day fears or everyday worries that manifest into obstacles of social or psychological proportions.

Book i : The Dark Transmutations in Our Night Time
Overture: Change
Themes: the fool, the adventurer, the apprentice, one, unity, beginnings.

Book ii : The Alchemal Quandary
Overture : Love
Themes : the lovers, act two, tragedy, plot progression, breaking, division.

Book iii : The Epoch Wake
Overture : Rebirth
Themes : mortality, the wake, the end, the crossroads, process, decay, beginnings, reprise.

Alchemy is the core concept for this series of writings. It is a philosophy that, at its rudimentary level, is a study of change. And each of us, as an individual person, experiences change in every fleeting moment we encounter. Alchemy is a tool for change, like our emotions are a tool for resolving our daily transitions from one state to another.

glossary

syn•drome — Symptoms that together are characteristic of a specific disorder; Related or coincident events; A characteristic pattern of behavior that indicates a particular, predictable, social condition under certain circumstances.

trans•mu•ta•tion — The state, act, or instance of transformation; From Physics: Transformation of one element into another by one or a series of nuclear reactions; From Alchemy: The conversion of a base metal into precious metal, such as lead to gold.

al•chemi•cal — Alchemy: A medieval chemical philosophy aimed at the transmutation of base metals, the discovery of the panacea (the 'All Cure'), the universal solvent (alkahest) that could dissolve any material property, and the preparation of the elixir of longevity postponing death.

quan•dary — A situation from which extrication is difficult especially an unpleasant or trying one; such as a predicament or plight; State of uncertainty or perplexity especially as a choice between equally unfavorable options.

ep•och — A particular period of time marked by distinctive features or events; In Astronomy, the mean longitude of a planet as seen from the sun at such an instant or date; In Physics, the displacement from zero at zero time of a celestial body undergoing simple harmonic motion.

wake — To become cognizant; brought to a state of awareness or alertness; A watch or vigil over the body of a deceased person before burial; The path or course of anything that has passed or preceded.

cadaver — The body of an inanimate or passed being; the deceased.

candor/candid — Freedom from bias; open expression without restraint or restrictions.

clandestine — Secret actions or diversions.

congenital — Disorder developed in utero; existing at or before birth.

conical — Geometric resemblance of a deep or shallow cone.

contraptions — Allegory usage, emphasis of being trapped within our own mechanical devices one creates themselves.

incandescent — Bright or brilliant light and heat.

listless — Restless; a body that must take to motion.

manifesto — A scripture or series of writings of a specific intent to educate social classes or persons; to sway those to your argument of intent.

marker — Where a cadaver lies; like a stone, pyre, ash, body, or tomb.

marriage — From alchemy, the meeting of two elements as they become one.

memento mori — From Latin vernacular, 'remember that you must die' ; an item, event, or symbol that serves as a reminder of mortality, limits, and death.

monsters — Manifestations of emotional states; apparition of our true nature or selves.

night / nite — A space for dreaming; The hours after solar failure until its return; represented by dusk, twilight, nightfall, midnight, gloam, evenfall, and crepuscule.

notorious — Unfavorably known; often a type of anti-fame or infamy.

occipital — The lower rear plate of the cranium situated at the back of the skull.

palpation — Examination or healing through touch.

panacea — Know as the 'All Cure' in alchemy, a tool or elixir that can heal anything; in modern vernacular, the magic bullet.

pander — A mediator in amorous intrigues; to caters to or profit from the weaknesses or vices of others.

pedagogues — Teacher or educator; instructor of a pedantic or dogmatic nature.

placebo — False remedy; sugar pills; psychological panacea or cure.

prestige — Distinct reputation upheld by an individual or group of others.

salient — Prominent events that stand out in memory versus monotonous actions; shocking, interruptive, exciting, or shaping events that remain in memory and cause critical change.

seem/seeming — Appearance; in replacement of lines of stitching.

skein — A succession or series of similar or interrelated things.

spite — Negative desire to do harm.

sunder — To sever or divide.

tián cǎo — From Chinese vernacular for sweet grass; tall, sweetly fragrant herb that preoccupies fields, especially in mid to late summer.

vellum — Thin parchment made from skin.

ventricle — Title of the two lower chambers on each side of the heart that receive blood from the atria and in turn forces it into the arteries of a body.

wolves — an allegory for girls/women.

index of First lines

index of first lines

author notations

It is likely at this point you are still curious about either the work, the words, or the author.

The work…

So, in your hands is something tangible. Other than the previous synopsis listed, the intent behind all of this writing has a lot more in the background than just themes, personal journals, and words.

Concepts and ideas often are intangible, and without putting it in print, they often are just sounds and phrases in our minds during the late hours of any given day.

It is not ideas that get us through the night, often they haunt us. However, it's the expectation, the thrall, or the need for a form of encouragement and satisfaction that guides our resolve.

Each work is a photograph, a type of still-life, or a little play that has been acted out or daydreamed. These painted scenes we all have on our minds that act out our hopes and fears.

author notations

The words…

I've always found inspiration from words and imagery, the concepts or strong willed beliefs of others. Often, in the dark, late at lonely hours, are these little words that hold us together and get us through another day.

These words come from friends and family, music idols, or intellectuals, humanitarians or media pedagogues. The best of us, the people we want to be and can in fact become; it's something in the human spirit perhaps.

My writing or 'language' that I've developed over the last ten years is built on metaphors, visions, or allegories I had previously created. These scenes are part real-life, part lyrical, and part fiction, in the most triumphant fashion possible.

Encouraging words mean more than the wounds we wear; that type of constant negativity and doubt each of us often carry, eating away our consciousness.

Encouraging words hold us up, and give us the will to do something inspiring, something compassionate and generous, or just get ourselves through one more day.

author notations

The author…

The artist and author of many web published works, designs, and creations, Bryan McLean is a fresh new author with visionary perceptions.

Raised and educated in Ontario, and has lived in various locations and worked for various corporations all across Canada.

Writing content and poetry for over fifteen years, originally trained as a fine artist, and is a student of culture, technology, music, literature, photography, as well as spirituality.

Bryan is a literary artist that brings us dark, exciting writing in a deep language that shows all of us as a generation fighting to live under great transition.

"I hope my words, although some of which may be encrypted and encoded, find you inspired to compassion, to creation, or just get you through one more long night."

www.ingramcontent.com/pod-product-compliance
Ingram Content Group UK Ltd.
Pitfield, Milton Keynes, MK11 3LW, UK
UKHW020219250726
13967UKWH00001B/94

9 781257 626281